© 1998 Franklin Watts
96 Leonard Street
London
EC2A 4RH

First American edition 1998 by
Franklin Watts
A Division of Scholastic Inc.
Sherman Turnpike
Danbury, CT 06816

ISBN 0-531-14497-6 (lib. bdg.)      0-531-15354-1  (pbk.)

A copy of the Cataloging-in-Publication Data is available
from the Library of Congress

Printed in Belgium

Editor: Kyla Barber
Art Director: Robert Walster
Designer: Diane Thistlethwaite
Illustrator: Teri Gower

Picture credits: Fiat: p12; Hutchison: p14 (Nancy Durrell McKenna); Honda: p10,
p11; Image Bank: p6, p19, p25 (Frank Whitney); Honda: p10, p11; Panos p6-7 (Jean-
Léo Dugast); QA Photos Ltd: cover, p18-19; Robert Harding: P8-9 (Kelly Harriger),
p13 (Scott Barrow, Int'l Stock), p22-23 (Liaison Int.); Zefa: p5, p15, p16-17 (Mathis),
p20-21 (Deuter), p23, p27; Rex: p24-25.

# MACHINES AT WORK

# On the Move

## Henry Pluckrose

# W
# FRANKLIN WATTS
## A Division of Scholastic Inc.
NEW YORK • LONDON • HONG KONG • SYDNEY
DANBURY, CONNECTICUT

People can travel on foot.
But it takes a long time
to get from place to place.

Machines help people
travel more quickly
and carry heavy loads.

A bicycle is
a machine.

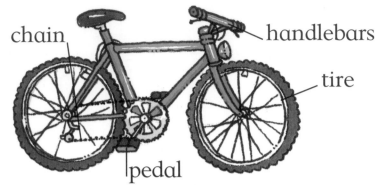

chain

handlebars

tire

pedal

The faster you pedal,
the faster you move.

You do not need to
pedal a motorcycle.

It has an engine that
makes the wheels go around.

Why is this person
wearing a helmet?

Cars have four wheels,
and the passengers sit inside.
Cars can travel very fast.

But when the roads are busy, a car
trip can seem slow and boring.

When lots of people want
to go to the same place,
they can travel together
on a bus or coach.

They can even
travel by streetcar.

Cars, buses, and coaches,
vans, and trucks
all use roads.

car fumes

They give off fumes that
pollute the air we breathe.

Trains run on specially
built railway tracks.

# Some trains travel below ground.

Trains have metal wheels
that fit onto the railway tracks.

Sometimes we need to travel across water.

Hovercraft

Ferry boats have space for trucks, coaches, cars, and people.

The ferry doors open to let the vehicles drive on.

FREMONT

Airplanes are machines that fly.
A jumbo jet can carry
more than 300 passengers.

The shape of an
airplane's wings and tail
helps it take off.

A helicopter is also a flying machine.

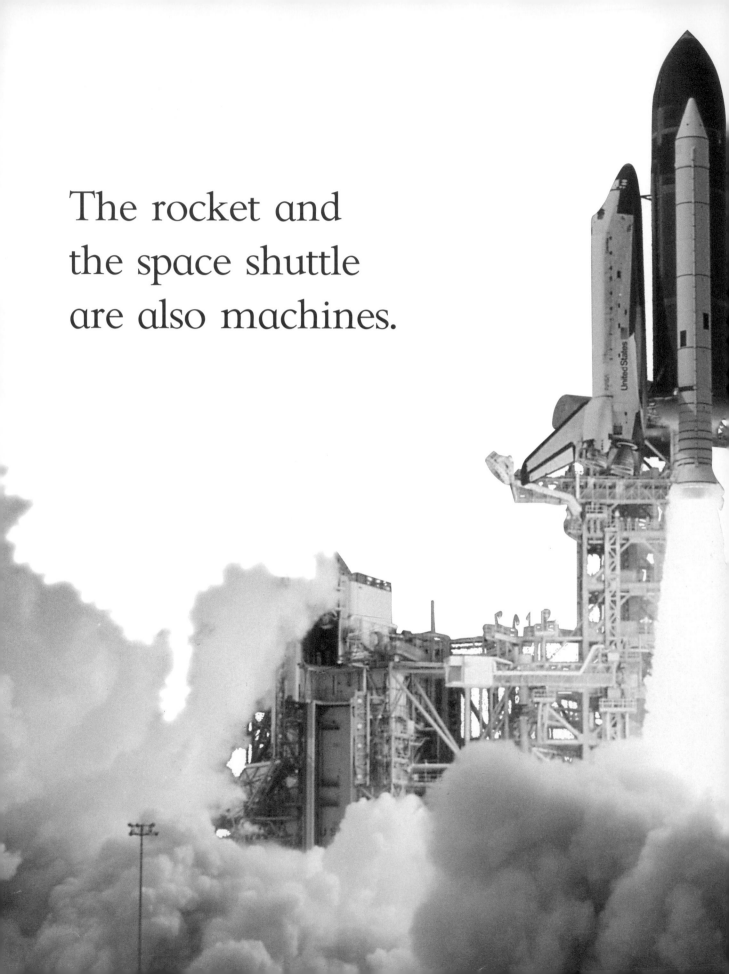

The rocket and
the space shuttle
are also machines.

The space shuttle carries astronauts into space and brings them safely back to Earth.

Some people find it
difficult to walk.
What machines
can help them?

Wheelchairs
cannot go up
or down stairs.
They need
special ramps.

bicycle

Hovercraft

# Glossary

**bicycles** have two wheels and two pedals.

**buses** pick up people at bus stops.

**coaches** carry people on long road trips.

**ferries** carry people, cars, and trucks across water.

**hovercrafts** take people and cars across water.

**motorbikes** have two wheels and an engine.

**space shuttles** take astronauts into space.

**streetcars** run on special tracks.

# Index

wheelchair

car fumes